L'HEURE BLEUE

OR

THE JUDY POEMS

ELISA GABBERT

L'HEURE BLEUE

also by Elisa Gabbert

The French Exit (2010)

The Self Unstable (2013)

L'Heure Bleue
or
The Judy Poems

Elisa Gabbert

Black Ocean
Boston · Detroit · Chicago

Black Ocean
P.O. Box 52030
Boston, MA 02205
blackocean.org

Cover Art and Design by Abby Haddican | abbyhaddican.com
Book Design by Nikkita Cohoon | nikkita.co

ISBN 978-1-939568-1-75

Library of Congress Cataloging-in-Publication Data

Names: Gabbert, Elisa, author.
Title: L'Heure bleue or The Judy poems / Elisa Gabbert.
Description: Boston : Black Ocean, [2016]
Identifiers: LCCN 2016027711 | ISBN 9781939568175 (pbk. : alk. paper)
Classification: LCC PS3607.A227 A6 2016 | DDC 811/.6--dc23
LC record available at https://lccn.loc.gov/2016027711

FIRST EDITION

Contents

II.

I loved him so much, it was a kind of torture.

—Judy, *The Designated Mourner,* Wallace Shawn

Perennial suffering has as much right to expression as a tortured man has to scream; hence it may have been wrong to say that after Auschwitz you could no longer write poems. But it is not wrong to raise the less cultural question whether after Auschwitz you can go on living—especially whether one who escaped by accident, one who by rights should have been killed, may go on living. His mere survival calls for the coldness, the basic principle of bourgeois subjectivity, without which there could have been no Auschwitz; this is the drastic guilt of him who was spared. By way of atonement he will be plagued by dreams such as that he is no longer living at all.

—Theodor Adorno, *Negative Dialectics*

Introduction

A few years ago, I invited some friends—local writers—to my apartment for cocktails. I didn't really know Elisa or her partner, the novelist John Cotter, very well at all. I knew and admired Elisa's first collection of poetry, *The French Exit*, but I had only spoken to her and John a few times at various poetry readings around town. They had recently moved to Denver from Boston, and they quickly made themselves a part of a vibrant community of poets in their new city.

At one point I found myself talking to John about theater. We both, it turned out, had been serious students of theater and had worked as actors and directors in our younger days. I don't remember how it came up, but we discovered we shared an affinity for the plays of Wallace Shawn, in particular *The Designated Mourner*. John recalled seeing Shawn at a bookstore in Manhattan, running to the drama section and grabbing a copy of the play for him to sign, which, I think, he did graciously

A week or two after that party, I was sitting in Elisa and John's living room, in front of an imposing wall of books, with a glass of wine in one hand and a copy of the play in the other. I read the part of Jack; Elisa read Judy, his wife; and John read Howard, Judy's father. Reading the play that evening felt remarkably natural. It felt to me like we were on to something that could potentially be incredibly fulfilling, artistically, and it felt *good*. We decided that we were going to mount a production. Once a week for a year, we met to "rehearse," if you can call it that. Our meetings were quite unlike any rehearsal process in which I'd participated before. Each week, the three of us sat around a table drinking wine, reading the play, discussing it, arguing about it. We talked for hours each evening about our characters' relationships to each other, their backstories, the politics in which they were entangled—in short, we spent a year becoming deeply intimate with this difficult little play. After a year, we began to perform it. We performed it a number of times, in people's living rooms, in art galleries—anywhere we could gather a few people to watch us.

The Designated Mourner takes place in an unnamed, fictitious country ruled over by an increasingly fascist oligarchy. It seemed to us to be a kind of strange mix of New York and Pinochet's Chile, a place where literary and artistic culture were thriving but coming under attack. In the play, the lower classes are beginning to rebel against the ruling class, and this causes the ruling class to take action against not only the rebels, but also against those they feel might incite rebellious behavior. This means, of course, that those in power begin going after artists and intellectuals. Howard, a well-known poet and essayist, is a central figure among these artists and intellectuals, and he becomes a target.

Howard's daughter, Judy, was married to Jack, an under-achieving English professor who was initially a kind of aspiring disciple of Howard, but later started to reject Howard's "high-brow" ways. Most likely, Jack's pulling away from Howard was a result of the fact that he and Judy were guilty by association in the eyes of those in power, and he was afraid. Jack leaves his wife and her father to live a more "low-brow" life. Eventually, Howard and Judy are both executed by the government, and Jack finds himself the last of their intellectual circle alive—the "designated mourner."

Throughout our rehearsal process, Elisa (who played her part brilliantly, in spite of the fact that she constantly reminded us she was "not an actor") often voiced a frustration with the way her character, Judy, was written. The character, she felt, lacked a depth that the male characters had. Within the text of the play, Judy seemed relatively underdeveloped, shallow. I think, like any good actor, Elisa began exploring the mind and history of the character in a much more nuanced way. She had been living with Judy for a year and had been imagining her unwritten life; she had been imagining Judy's feelings toward her father and toward her husband with a level of complexity that the play does not. It made her performance as sophisticated as any I've seen by a "professional" actor.

However, Elisa is a poet. It stands to reason, then, that she would begin thinking through Judy in the form of poetry. A short time after we stopped performing *The Designated Mourner*, Elisa started to write what would become *L'Heure Bleue, or The Judy Poems*. This is how it happened, in her words:

All I know is that once I was sitting in the audience at a poetry reading, which is one of the places that I often get ideas for poems . . . and I suddenly had the first couple of lines from the book come to me. They're still the first lines of the book. And I wrote them down, and I was like, Oh—I should write in Judy's voice.

These are the words she wrote:

I'm not in love with Jack.

I have a crush on Jack.

Jack is my husband, who left me.

I certainly don't think a reader needs to be familiar with *The Designated Mourner* to find value in these poems; they are remarkable on their own. I feel lucky, though, to have been witness to the early stages of their development. I also feel lucky to be able to read and reread this new collection from such a vibrant and important contemporary poet.

—Aaron Angello

I'm not in love with Jack.

I have a crush on Jack.

Jack is my husband, who left me.

"Absence makes the heart grow fonder"
is a silly way of putting the truth,
that rejection is seductive.

I.

Am I the sea?

Am I the sea
or do I hate the sea?

Am I befallen?
I feel befallen.
I once imagined

dropping my keys
down a grate and it's sharp
as a memory.

For a week
Jack calls everything magic.
That's magic, he says. *It's magic!*

He's crazy but I agree.
It's Shakespearean.
There are messages

in some trash and bits of twig
on the step, the pigeons
who are always together—

three of them, a conspiracy.
Whose pigeons?
Whose magic?

Jack always feels like someone is watching.

So we turn it into a game.
We do things for their benefit.

We invent a code name for suicide,
"The Attractive Option,"
and refer to it often.

Emerson said,
For every minute you are angry
you lose sixty seconds of happiness.

But he also said, *The purpose of life*
is not to be happy.

I say to Jack,
Life makes it impossible
not to waste your life.

Speech is a charade, of course,
but sometimes I think things
for their benefit. An idea
is part of the persona.

I'm interested in the point
where the game crosses over,
where he is laughing
and I am afraid.

At the poetry reading,

I scribble in a notebook.

The girl with the bee tattoo on her back
satisfies my need for "luminous detail."

Dusk falls. *L'heure bleue.* Black trees
silhouetted over indigo sky
is my favorite sight,

a streetlight unfurling
its liquid red beam.

I maintain a certain level
of detachment like a buzz.

A man makes eye contact.

There are times when desire seems
to transfer. He communicates desire;
I am infected by desire.

It's the worst kind of desire—
too thin a film
between desire and reality.

Some days I can't escape the feeling

that something is touching me,
that I'm inescapably touching myself.
This is my *body*, I think, repulsed.

I don't want to be beautiful
so much as remembered
as beautiful.

The past is inherently interesting:
patina of mystery, low resolution.
Ugly people are beautiful
in old pictures.

We will be beautiful too,
but forgotten.

I go outside again.
I stand and breathe
by the honeysuckle bush
until the honeysuckle has no scent.

A walk helps a little, a pause

where I am moving

and other things stay the same,
or have less distinguishing detail.

The sky in this mood
is more supple. Not quality of life,

but quality of suffering.
Just to say "I suffer" helps.

A dog rubs its heavy black body
against my thigh,

thrusts its head between my legs.
I hate this automatic shame.

We go to see the glass flowers

at the museum of natural history. Outside
the grass is unseasonably green.

I tell Jack it's a feature
of the simulation.

Do grasshoppers really
have butterfly wings?

Or is this an embellished version
of the world as it was,
an unreliable memory?

The museum is boring
and closes too soon,
and it's too bright
even though it looks like rain.

Maybe the dead raccoon
we almost killed again today
was there for a reason.

Jack, I ask, *what does it mean,*
in terms of magic.

I'm not interested in art today.

Art stinks of wealth.

In the museum everyone seems
to be glancing, looking
to be watched.

First wealth as beauty,
then wealth as irreverence.
(Should art do no harm?)

Whatever I wear,
having money
makes me look rich.

Money is potential
energy, an aggravation.
A migraine

is glamourous,
but this is a common headache—
dull, not all-consuming.

I place a journal by my bed.
In "the cold light of day,"

what I wrote looks like poetry.
And the light of day is warm.

The *melo-* in *melodramatic*

means soft. Like *nagging*, it's a way
of calling me a woman.

Love is loathing
ourselves, but not the other.
Ha! My character

knows things I don't,
can see all the errors.

To put myself to sleep,
I think time is passing through me,
not me through it.

Lying in bed I watch
one blade of the fan spin
instead of the whole blur.

There's an end of pipe
on the ceiling that looks
like an upside-down hat,

an open eye—
what does it know?

I'll let my thoughts happen;
figure out what to do
with them later.

(Important
not to confuse my life
with the world.)

Jack is jealous

of our scientist friend.
He comes over for dinner

and eats a bowl of cereal.
Cereal is a local maximum,
he says, trying to impress me.

Jack can see it's working.
He says the scientist is my type:
tall and an asshole.

He's right, I say, *You're right*,
but the scientist is sweet
beneath his ego.

He doesn't care about looks
so I can be alluring
without embarrassment.

The scientist: *There are now more deaths*
from suicide than car accidents.
You can't harvest those bodies for organs.

Jack says, *Ah! Progress!*,
lights a cigarette.

The day the torture report comes out,

Jack can't suppress a smirk—
he seems to enjoy this dark energy.

I didn't read the report.
I assume it involves
descriptions of people being tortured.

A boy I knew in college, at 22,
was already worried his mind was going.

He was working on some kind of algorithm.
He wore orange blossom cologne,
said it calmed him.

The neighbor's black cat
is posing in the window again,
a pure silhouette.

Whether something strikes me
as obvious or profound
depends entirely on my mood.

Is that true?

When I say what I think,

someone always tells me they agree
or disagree, which ruins
the thought for me.

In this way, little by little,
I forget what I believe.
My memories seem as false
as an alternate reality,

a reflection in a window
I used to pretend was an older,
more sophisticated self—
a woman with pain, in sunglasses.

The thrill I felt
when my grandfather died:
finally some meaning,
or, at least, novelty.

Only at the funeral,
when I saw my mother crying,
did I experience sadness. No—
it's more that I was frightened.

I am not very clever today.

There's a strange rain falling:
slow drops, yellow sky.

The scientist makes us take
personality tests.
This seems beneath him.

Given two options,
I'm troubled by the worry
I could get this wrong:

You feel involved watching TV soaps.
You trust reason more than feelings.

For Jack, it's a chance
to build a new Jack.
Every type is plausible:

The Warrior. The Diplomat.
Why not just choose?

I'm stuck on a graffito
I saw this morning
in the café bathroom—

a simple kind of thought,
but I had thought it mine.

The scientist is oddly optimistic,

another way of being contrary.

When Jack and I complain all night
he wanders away, opens a book
and abruptly shuts it.

He says, *Let's make a list
of things we love without reservation.*

Five minutes later, Jack is immersed
in this childish exercise.

I am hungry and can only think of food:

Pork roasted over cherry branches.
Affogato. Anything
drunken or drowned.

The scientist leaves
without reading his list.

Jack keeps writing.
It is mostly music.

To avoid Jack when he's sad—

what he indulgently calls "the blues"—
I say, *You're catastrophizing again*,

a word I learned from his therapist.
It's part of the new cruelty.

Jack quote-unquotes Emerson:
Truth is shrill as a fife. I'm sure
Emerson hated women.

I'm unsure of the verb:
Have I wifed Jack
or is Jack wifing me?

I revive an old shirt
that shows off my clavicle.
Vanity is my last vanity,

and I reserve the right
to wear lipstick in the house
and smear it on the cups.

Here everything is admissible,
my silence as weaponry,
my too much perfume.

A little drunk in the park with Jack

and he's making me laugh.
It's hard to remember last week

how I saw no point to this.
I don't remember the feeling,
just the words as I spoke them

to myself. Like wishing for snow
when it gets too hot,
though I hate the cold.

By the second bottle
the jokes are ahead of us;
they want to tell us what we think.

When you lie down on the hill,
you know you're on the outside
of the world, with all of space

below you. The clouds blow by:
What is the point of this?
This isn't a place

I can stay in.
When he moves to kiss me
I say, *Don't.*

Art should be easy—

can't I create whatever I want?
It begins that way.

But then, whims. Then
boredom, failure.

They say that things will always change.
It feels like they're changing
backwards, with no surprises.

What are you thinking about?
Jack used to ask. My thoughts
don't coalesce into thoughts,

just static, and something-
something about death,
which has grown quite boring

and automatic. Who knows
what they want?
My thoughts aren't exact

so they don't coalesce
into my preferred syntax.

He hates the silence,
which I think is perfect.

When we argue about war,

I say I'm a pacifist
and he looks for a loophole.

He brings up Hitler, genocide—
these noble causes.

The problem I have
is distinguishing between atrocities:
the genocide on one hand

and on the other
atomic bombs (their eyeballs melted),
torture, women and children

raped and murdered
for the greater good.
It's like the difference between

a billion and a trillion—
I believe they are different
but can't conceive of it.

The moral imperative
justifies the amoral,
the technically lesser atrocity.

I think citizens don't have to think
like countries.

Names of girls.

Names of paintings.
Names of horses.

I can't decide which
I prefer: the struggle
or the boredom.

We have little to say, so Jack asks,
What was the best thing
that happened to you today?

Then on to the worst:
"The Rose & the Thorn."

I burned my finger on the oven
this morning, burnt
to a blister—

it's good to remember
how much it hurts.

"A war-torn country."
This repetition, this reportage.

II.

There are certain points in time

that everyone remembers.
It is not just me.
This was one of those points.

We had crossed into
November. I spoke
of my desire. I said desire

but I meant longing.
Desire is despair
with sex mixed in.

A crossing of levels.
We drew overlapping circles
on the inside cover

of a paperback novel:
the new & the interesting.
A narrow eye.

After dinner: dessert,
and then another drink,
then I touch myself

if I can't fall asleep:
always the need
for some final pleasure.

Afterwards
I lose all interest in sex;
it is not intellectual.

I wonder if hares
are bored all the time
and terrified of death.

After a seizure,

my epileptic friend says
he recognizes strangers.

Every face looks familiar,
the only sign that something's wrong.

I feel this way all the time now.
Petit mal—little bad.
My *eigengrau* isn't gray, but red.

The mind zags diagonal,
thinking variations
on its own thoughts,

desire paths
where the grass is worn down.

I don't care about sex
and that, my friend says,
makes me sexy.

Oh, I say,
I would have liked
to have had a sister.

When I was a girl,

setting the table,
I was very careful

where I placed the odd knife,
the faded napkin
or the chipped plate.

Whomever got it,
I imagined they would die.
That was my power.

I usually gave it to my brother.
Later, my father.
(But never my mother.)

Older, I'd take it for myself.
(The prophecy unfulfilled,
my bravery went unnoticed.)

Whether or not I believe in fate
is academic—fate trumps belief,

the relentless happening
continues to happen.

When things get stuck,
I leave the house,
a spell for the random.

Lately before bed

I hear voices—

muffled, overlapping,
like messages
on a worn-out tape.

I look up
"auditory hallucinations."

I read an essay
about "aura," the premonition
of a migraine. Of course,

I think—the suffering
that comes before

real suffering,
trivial in retrospect.

They are asking questions

but not for me to answer.
I'm the third person.

I wake up with bumps

all over my legs.
They don't hurt or itch

but are very ugly.
I can think of nothing
but my ruined legs.

Shostakovich
would "quote" himself,
mockingly—

no way to know
which parts were
the real S.

When I can't sleep
I try to imagine
impossible things,

to force myself
into a dream. The mind
keeps slipping

back into simplicity, memory—
not consciousness, just memory
in real time.

I go to the movies,

though I hate movies.
I always cry at the movies.

It seems important
that imaginary people are happy.

No one asks why I never had children.
I guess never is a word for after
you're dead, as in, *I never loved you*.
I imagine saying it at his grave.

I imagine him with a grave, the way
I imagine having a daughter.

She is always a daughter, never a son,
and never a baby, always 7 or 8.

(Then you must not want a baby?)

Nostalgia is the only cure

for nostalgia—

listen to old jazz singers,
remember old lovers,

literally ad nauseam.
That'll show me.

I wanted to be one of those
austere beauties

who end up with neurotic men
who think they have to drink to relax

and are yet more irrational
after two manhattans.

They didn't kill me
but they made me meaner.

This convention of saying we're "fine"

is backwards. Not fine
is the default, and saying so feels better.

I've been reading bad poetry,
taking everything literally. It is dusk
on Sunday, therefore we're blue.

You can't read in a bar
without seeing yourself reading:
in the half-silvered glass,

in the eyes of the women
who see you looking at them too—

Behind the thorny pink
Close wall of blossom'd may.

The waiter remembers me, calls me *Honey*.
We're in the window of knowing
between fondness and contempt

but we can't stay there.
Somehow I'll fail.

Just like the future,

the past branches out
into infinite possibilities.

I keep trying to look back
at a different path.

Then comes the sense
that it doesn't matter.
Alack, alack, alack.

I consult the list of things
that reliably make me happy
(or forget that I'm not):

Driving, with music.
Painting (if it's good).
Poker, Hearts, Gin.

The mind rejects them.
Chooses the image.

In one of those blank

spaces of the day

I lost the little notebook
where I was collecting
place-name phrases:

California stop.
Giving it English.
Irish goodbye.

There is so much time.
No wonder we're unable
to account for it all,

to reconstruct it later.
I flip through a book
called *History in Pictures*

but they're only pictures—
no one event
is more historical than the next.

It's pseudointellectual
to dwell on the arbitrary
in any distinction.

Intelligence without wisdom—
that's what I despise.

Jack would say,
Even crows have a theory of mind.

When I read old entries in my journal,

it's easy to imagine they were written
by someone else—someone

I've grown fond of. This is why
I write down my mistakes. Or some days,
a single word: *Resistance. Relief.*

Today it's as though
I'm reliving a moment
for the first time.

Jack gave me a book of haiku
and told me to look for the *kigo*.
I tried crossing them out,

making my own Sapphos:

Even though afar
A feeling of   comes
From those

Then I find a Basho that is only *kigo*—

Archipelago
Archipelago
Archipelago

—an example of his "speechlessness
at the Ah-ness of things,"
the footnote tells me.

I can't improve on this.

On TV, people walk into your house

unannounced. They go upstairs
and right into the bedroom.

I wish this would happen to me.
I leave my doors unlocked.

I try to live my life
as a character—eat pancakes
for breakfast, dab at an ugly painting.

There's a line of empty bottles
in the garage: Campari and red wine.
I'm cultivating habits for my biographer.

With Jack it came out wry,
but now it sounds self-pitying.
I pity myself the more!

I like to think of someone
working on me, years from now—
an archaeologist, a doctor,
someone to figure it out.

Something about fish

that is melancholy—everyone
at the koi pond knows this.

And morning, just by sound,
is macabre.

You construct a self
out of things only a few
people see every day.

The public has primacy
over the private—it pains me
to admit. But privacy

can't just be about shame.
I want to have things
I'm proud of to myself.

How you are alone—
it's almost erotic.
Is that taboo?

Wake up in the dark,
une fille en aiguilles,
a girl in needles.

They flick away.

I don't fantasize about sex,

just kissing him. Somehow,
I don't embody me. I watch it
in the third person.

It's like looking in a mirror,
but we're out of sync.
I don't want her to see me.

Jack asked, *Why are you just lying there?*
I hadn't noticed. When he was here,
I found him a distraction.

I have discovered

that two dull activities
become interesting together;

take cleaning while
listening to Brahms.

A nothing little
snow outside.

Eyelashes in a library book.

With no other body
to look at, I look at
my own body.

I remember taking pictures
of myself and waiting
for the film to develop.

I dislike what I see,
but remain arrogant.

I'm happiest when I live simply,

but they like me when I'm complex.

"They" seem indistinct
from the landscape; I perceive no edges.
Birds in an Escher tessellation.

When it snows I think of Jack,
because Jack loved the snow, coming down
in blurs. I see geese on the lake

and think of Jack. It's a new park
but the geese are the same, I'm sure
they're the same geese. Unmajestic,

they shit and wander
meaninglessly, in tandem
with the midges. I don't know

the present tense of Jack.
He had no sense of constancy.

If the pattern isn't random
it's opaque.

In the too bright

performance space
I stare at a girl's hair,
its gleam and wave,

and want nothing
more from life. No other
forms of beauty.

Boredom trumps everything.
If you're bored enough
you'll never die.

I start to cry and then
get bored; I excuse myself

to look in the mirror.
Abhorrent.

I like Dickinson's face
but not her poetry.

What I like or don't
is boring, a tyranny,
even to me.

I would say to Jack,
What do you *want*?,
but what I meant was,

What do *I* want?
What do *I* want?

As it is, I feel nothing

at the Holocaust Museum.

We've left the propaganda section
but it still looks like propaganda.

The woman next to me is crying
openly. I walk away. I imagine

that the photographs are art,
muse on the subjectivity of the artist,

on buttons as punctum. I imagine
I am perfecting failure.

There's a photo of Jack
I look at again and again—

not for remove.
To get closer.

One fact about Jack:

He had music playing
all the time. Being distracted

makes some things more interesting.
I would try to see him
with my side-mind.

I trace the caning
on the backs of the chairs,
if I'm bored at least

I'm thinking. Why do I always
have to be there, though?
In my thoughts?

Dreams are like a movie:
just watching strangers,
but intimately. Quiet and apart.

I want to know
what anyone thinks about
all the time.

Adorno's famous line

about poetry after Auschwitz
was meaningless out of context,

Jack would oft remind me:
To quote Adorno after Auschwitz
is barbaric.

Once over dinner I misheard
my father and everafter have referred
to Jack's "violet moods."

In the late afternoon,
coming out of the library

into mean winter light
(not bright but in your eyes)

he would place his hand
on the small of my back
and "all was forgiven."

Why can't I simulate
the feeling with my own hand?

That sudden, warm blue?

I have thought enough

about my father. I have tried

the Buddhist trick of "watching"
your thoughts float by

but my thoughts are not images or floating
sentences until I try to watch them,

and then they become more real,
something I can remember,

like a color on a map.
Heightened with place and time.

And where am I watching from?
Outside, or further inside?

I find an old typed up paper:

words I don't remember
about things I don't know.

In what sense did I write them?

I wish there were a devil to bargain with.

I try and fail to ruin my life.

Why is it, that such little beauty
should keep me satisfied?

I knew he would go.

And then, one day, he went.
In a way, nothing's changed.

There is no risk now
of repeating myself.
In fact I prefer it.

My friends keep talking about
some celebrity death,
a controversial writer.
I can't hide my jealousy.

All my life I've had this perverse
desire for what I don't want—
I think of the worst alternative
and then wish for it.

Things have to pass through
the present to get to the past,
where they can be cherished.

I could know him, and like him,

without understanding,
like liner notes to a jazz album.

But liking doesn't lead to love.
You switch to a different axis.

A self-indulgent misery
is best, a cathartic performance
I perform myself.

I read that happy people have
an inaccurate sense of time.
The descent as slow falling. The dead
don't get any more dead.

When remembering him,
I'm never lonely.

The day after Christmas,

a late morning walk.

Otherworldly mist
over the foothills.

A family of geese, startlingly
beautiful when quiet.

Damp earth—when it's damp
it feels like earth, not ground.

Black feathers,
black ruffled edges

of some kind of tarp
under the landscaping.

Most fossil fuel
does not come from dinosaurs

but sea plankton.
All of these "facts," garbled

the first time by Jack
and now half-remembered,

surfacing at random.
(True randomness

is rare, though.)
Like pockets of air.

Acknowledgements

Thanks to the editors of the journals where some of these poems originally appeared: *Apartment Poetry, Denver Poetry Map, Diagram, Guernica, Harvard Review, Jubilat, Linebreak, Okey-Panky, Pank, PEN Poetry Series, Phantom Limb, Phoebe,* and *Public Pool.* Thanks to Andrew Ridker for including an excerpt in *Privacy Policy: The Anthology of Surveillance Poetics.*

Special thanks to my early readers, Teju Cole, Liz Hildreth, and Kathleen Rooney; to Abby Haddican and Nikkita Cohoon for their care with this book's design; and to my editors, Carrie Olivia Adams and Janaka Stucky.

This book is dedicated to the members of Denver Poets Theater, Aaron Angello and John Cotter.

Notes

L'heure bleue is French for "the blue hour." It is also the name of a perfume created in 1912 by Jacques Guerlain.

The italicized lines in "This convention of saying we're 'fine'" are from "Revelation" by Edmund Gosse.

The quoted lines in "When I read old entries in my journal" are from a footnote in *The Classic Tradition of Haiku* edited by Faubion Bowers.